Developing Personal & Interpersonal Responsibility

In Children & Youth with Emotional/Behavioral Disorders

Sylvia Rockwell   Santa Cuccio

Beth Kirtley   Gwen Smith

Pinellas County Public Schools

Lyndal M. Bullock & Robert A. Gable, *Series Editors*

The Council for Children with Behavioral Disorders, *Publisher*

About the Council for Children with Behavioral Disorders

CCBD is an international professional organization committed to promoting and facilitating the education and general welfare of children and youth with behavioral and emotional disorders. CCBD, whose members include educators, parents, mental health personnel, and a variety of other professionals, actively pursues quality educational services and program alternatives for persons with behavioral disorders, advocates for the needs of such children and youth, emphasizes research and professional growth as vehicles for better understanding behavioral disorders, and provides professional support for persons who are involved with and serve children and youth with behavioral disorders.

In advocating for the professionals in the field of behavioral disorders, CCBD (a division of The Council for Exceptional Children) endorses the Standards for Professional Practice and Code of Ethics adopted by the Delegate Assembly of The Council for Exceptional Children in 1983.

About This Monograph

Stock No. D5240, ISBN 0-86586-306-7

Printed in the United States of America

10   9   8   7   6   5   4   3   2

Contents

Foreword

This is the second mini-library series that addresses the needs of students identified as "seriously emotionally disturbed" or "emotionally/behaviorally disordered." As with the first series, the content stems from selected presentations at an international conference sponsored by the Council for Children with Behavioral Disorders (CCBD). These monographs are also a response to the reality that the number of children and youth who evidence challenging behavior is growing. These students manifest a range of social, academic, and behavior problems that test the skills of even the most capable classroom teachers. Educators and other professionals are struggling to find ways to deal successfully with the mounting challenges these students present.

Fortunately, as the number of problems increases, so too does the body of accumulated literature on practices of proven effectiveness for students with emotional/behavioral disorders (EBD). Drawing upon the expertise of CCBD members, we have assembled a seven-volume series of monographs that delve into some of the specific areas and programs for students with EBD and the education professionals who work with them:

- *Alternative Programs for Students with Social, Emotional, or Behavioral Problems*
  Mary Magee Quinn and Robert B. Rutherford, Jr.

- *Curriculum and Instruction Practices for Students with Emotional / Behavioral Disorders*
  Rex E. Schmid and William Evans, Editors

- *Developing Personal and Interpersonal Responsibility in Children and Youth with Emotional/Behavioral Disorders*
  Sylvia Rockwell, Santa Cuccio, Beth Kirtley, and Gwen Smith

- *Developing Social Competence in Children and Youth with Challenging Behaviors*
  Kristine J. Melloy, Carol A. Davis, Joseph H. Wehby, Francie R. Murry, and Jennifer Leiber

- *Enhancing Self-Respect: A Challenge for Teachers of Students with Emotional/Behavioral Disorders*
  Ann Fitzsimons-Lovett

- *Individual and Systemic Approaches to Collaboration and Consultation on Behalf of Students with Emotional/Behavioral Disorders*
  Robert A. Gable, George Sugai, Tim Lewis, J. Ron Nelson, Douglas Cheney, Stephen P. Safran, and Joan S. Safran

- *Teaching Children and Youth Self-Control: Applications of Perceptual Control Theory*
  John W. Maag

In these seven monographs, we have attempted to bring together information that addresses the needs of general and special educators, administrators, and other professionals who face the myriad challenges of children and youth at risk for or with EBD. We are grateful for the contributions of the monograph authors and hopeful that their efforts will prove useful to you in your work on behalf of students with EBD.

Lyndal M. Bullock
University of North Texas

Robert A. Gable
Old Dominion University

Series Editors

Introduction: Growing Up Responsible

1

Teaching children and youth to be trustworthy, disciplined, and accountable for their actions is a complex and lengthy process. From a child's earliest moments, impressions about the world begin to take shape. Initial lessons in responsibility are as basic as having one's needs for food, warmth, shelter, cleanliness, and touch met reliably. Erikson (1963) describes the infant's challenges during that first psychosocial stage in terms of trust and mistrust. Maslow (1962) defines the first two levels in his hierarchy of human needs as those required to sustain life, ensure physical security, and provide psychological safety. From these foundations, a general sense of well-being is established. The world can be trusted to respond in life-sustaining ways.

As children move into the toddler years, they face their first lessons in exerting and subjugating self-will. Erikson (1963) refers to this stage as a struggle between autonomy and shame or doubt. Protective boundaries in the environment must be monitored by adults during this period of growth. Toddlers explore indiscriminately, and their need for safety must be balanced with their need to exert self-will. Effectively establishing and maintaining protective boundaries and resolving the inevitable conflicts that arise as toddlers begin to assert themselves provides a basis for the child's first understandings of hope and responsibility.

The third stage, according to Erikson (1963), is marked by a sense of initiative built on the autonomy mastered during the previous stage. While autonomy, as often as not, took the form of defiance in the face of direct attempts by others to control the child, individual initiative can be seen in a propensity to plan and direct activities toward goals. These preschool years are filled with imitating adult roles and behaviors, exploring personal limits in active play, and taking great joy in all new accomplishments. Assisting adults in routine, age-appropriate chores takes on special meaning. The youngster is beginning to actively participate in Maslow's (1962) third level of functioning as evidenced by a sense of belonging. When a child oversteps the limits of his or her capacity to exert self-control, adults must provide protective boundaries once again to ensure physical safety as well as protection against undue feelings of guilt.

Children who are fortunate enough to have received adequate levels of support during those early years and who exhibit the traits necessary for overcoming the risk factors that might be present in their lives, enter school ready to engage in the challenges responsible, industrious youngsters enjoy. Rudimentary life stories are already forming in the minds of these very young children (Wood, 1996). They express a belief, clearly aligned with their actions, in themselves, their peers, and the adults in their world. Life has had a predictable, protective, sustaining pattern prior to their entry into school. They do not conceive of a world that is different.

Once students reach school age, a period of growth begins that is marked by a desire to earn recognition through production. Achievement in the formal as well as the informal educational expectations of society lead to a sense of industry. A child's failure to adequately meet demands at this time creates feelings of inferiority (Erikson, 1963). Families, communities, and schools contribute to the child's capacity for responsible thinking, feeling, and behaving. A quote from Marian Wright Edelman illustrates the power of the environment in shaping a child's life story.

> I was 14 years old the night my Daddy died. He had holes in his
> shoes but two children out of college, one in college, another in
> divinity school, and a vision he was able to convey to me as he

Developing Personal and Interpersonal Responsibility

lay dying in an ambulance that I, a young Black girl, could be and do anything; that race and gender are shadows; and that character, self-discipline, determination, attitude, and service are the substance of life.

I have always believed that I could help change the world because I have been lucky to have adults around me who did—in small and large ways. Most were people of simple grace who understood what Walter Percy wrote: You can get all A's and still flunk life. Giving up and 'burnout' were not part of the language of my elders. You got up every morning and did what you had to do and you got up every time you fell down and tried as many times as you had to get it done right. They had grit. (Edelman, 1992, pp. 7-8)

It is clear from Edelman's brief description of her early years that protective and supportive structures surrounded her from her first beginnings. She reports feeling loved and challenged through multiple experiences with family, friends, and community members. While she faced many hardships and obstacles, her earliest beliefs about herself reflected those of the adults who surrounded her with high expectations, an unwavering sense of hope for her and for the world at large, and an honest appraisal of what it would take to succeed. Her sense of personal and interpersonal responsibility as an adult has been built upon those childhood messages and experiences.

Many students with emotional/behavioral disorders (EBD) have not had such protective, predictable, supportive care. Other children have been carefully nurtured by loving families but exhibit EBD due to organic dysfunction. Whether the characteristics that present themselves in the classroom stem from biological disorders, inadequate care, neglect, acts of abuse, or a constellation of known and unknown causes, teaching students with EBD to be responsible is a complex process.

As students grow, they add more experiences to the life stories they construct. If the majority of their experiences have been unproductive, they will carry a set of beliefs with them that actively work against more direct efforts to teach social skills and manage surface behavior. In contrast to Edelman's story and as an illustration of the power of children's beliefs in the maintenance of their behaviors, an experience with a class of fourth and fifth grade boys with EBD is presented next. This experience, like the others in this monograph, are taken from the authors' real-life experiences with children with EBD but are not drawn from their current employment (unless directly specified) which is the Calvin A. Hunsinger School, a public school in Pinellas County, Florida. This center serves students with EBD in kindergarten through Grade 12. The following experience comes from the first author, Sylvia Rockell.

All of the boys in this class lived with parents who were either addicted to drugs or engaged in illegal activities. They told me often about shootings at night in their neighborhoods. According to them, all of the children who lived in their area went inside at dusk to play games or watch television. They remained flat on the floor each evening to escape bullets that might hit them from drive-by shootings. One child had watched his mother die when he was 5 years old. His stepfather had chopped off his mothers arms. It took the police several hours to talk the man into letting this child and his sister leave the house. Another boy witnessed a violent attack by his mother on his father's girlfriend. The father was having sex with his pregnant girlfriend in the parent's bedroom. When the mother came home and found them together, she stabbed the woman in the abdomen. The baby died.

I repeatedly attempted to discuss the benefits of maintaining a nonviolent classroom with this group. I told them that fighting was not a responsible way to handle anger and conflicts, but they had plenty to tell me about that. They told me about their lack of trust, their need to defend not only their honor but also their very existence. They challenged me to live just one day in their shoes. They were only 10 and 11 years old. In spite of my determination to run a safe and trustworthy program, they persisted in seeing danger and reasons for aggression at every turn. They cursed, threw furniture, smashed windows and other school property, and resorted to a group brawl on the lawn in front of the classroom on more than one occasion. They were so determined to prove to me that might is right.

While I could not totally change that belief in the short period of one school year, we did eventually establish a peaceful classroom. They learned to be responsible within the four protected walls of our environment. We cooked, read, wrote books, built model towns, sang, and talked. Our book and model town were placed on display in the school office. Our treats were shared with staff and other classes. We established a community of mutual respect, trust, and care that allowed those young men to be responsible with me and with each other. In order to accomplish that, multiple experiences over a period of months were developed to satisfy their needs for safety, trust, nurturing, protective and supportive boundaries, achievement, choices, and service to others.

Neither a behavior-management system nor a series of social skills lessons alone would have been enough. The students needed to be heard. And I needed to know what they were thinking. I could not even imagine living in such a terrifying environment. Even if they embellished some of the details and were less than accurate at times about all that they reported, their beliefs about themselves and others came through in our discussions. By listening to their stories, I gained a better understanding of how to meet their needs in ways that would make sense to them. They needed the same things that we all need — to feel safe, valued, strong, capable, and worthy. When past experiences have not lead to socially acceptable methods for meeting those needs, however, teaching personal and interpersonal responsibility is a tremendous challenge.

I would like to pretend that I began the year in that classroom with a clearly defined plan but the reality is I did not. The students' propensity to interpret every action as a threat was as wearing as it was disturbing. This group of children required diligently enforced controls on all acts of aggression within a structure that protected their needs to see themselves as strong and independent. I drew large boxes on the floor around their desks with chalk. Time-out was immediately enforced for any movement that extended out of their area. Academic work was carefully structured for student success. Anytime a student said, "I can't do this," I replied, "I will never ask you to do anything that can't be done. Tell me what you know. We'll go from there together."

Daily routines included negotiable and nonnegotiable items. A sense of power and control can be enhanced through opportunities to make choices and give suggestions. In spite of their limited abilities in the beginning to make responsible choices and provide appropriate input, carefully structured academic and affective lessons were offered that elicited such responses. Each of their names was posted on the chalkboard. Whenever possible, I asked for their opinions or hypotheses and recorded answers given next to their names.

Independent work was often assigned with a group project in mind. In the beginning, working together was impossible. Working alone to contribute to a class product allowed students the safety and sense of accomplishment they needed while encouraging them to take pride in group membership. As projects took shape, they were shared with the larger community of the school. Students received positive feedback from other teachers, administrators, and peers. Family members were encouraged to visit as well. Being strong, capable, and worthy extended beyond the ability to fight. Power, control, and achievement were possible through school appropriate behaviors. The group was finally able to function peacefully. I no longer drew boxes on the floor around their desks. They did not give up their belief that the world beyond the classroom was a threatening place. They still believed in violence. However, new choices were added to their repertoire and practiced daily although it must be said that the new did not by any stretch of the imagination erase the old.

When one of the students was asked in the spring of that school year what he had liked about the class, he said that the teacher did not want to talk about what he could not do — only what he could do. Students with EBD are often too aware of what they cannot do. Empowering them to become responsible members of a class, school, and community requires a balancing of their needs for attachment versus independence, autonomy versus external control, and initiative versus destruction or apathy. The things that we do for them, to them, and with them send powerful messages. Behavior-management techniques and social skills instruction are necessary building blocks but will not bring about desired results in isolation. Responsibility is a global and complex habit of thinking, feeling, and behav-

     Developing Personal and Interpersonal Responsibility

ing that emerges as individuals develop and interact with family, friends, school personnel, and the community.

Drawing on the literature and our own professional experiences, we provide in the next two chapters a brief overview of the characteristics and needs of children during the elementary school years and adolescence. An understanding of the typical milestones youth encounter as they develop personal and interpersonal skills is useful in planning productive interventions for students with EBD. Each chapter also includes examples of projects, programs, and interventions practitioners have implemented with positive results in school settings.

The Elementary School Years 2

All children need the protective and instructional benefits of a well-designed behavior-management system, direct social skills instruction, and authentic opportunities to practice those skills in reinforcing environments. When environmental demands are within students' repertoires, the lessons of personal and interpersonal responsibility are acquired with a minimum of concern. Unfortunately, children with EBD express a variety of unproductive beliefs and exhibit a range of socially unacceptable behavioral excesses and deficits that are not sanctioned by schools. Designing programs for them that inspire and instill a sense of responsibility provides educators with an extra measure of challenge. The next section provides some of the relevant developmental factors teachers can use when motivating students to modify their beliefs as well as their behaviors. It is followed by descriptions of strategies and materials practitioners have found to be effective.

Developmental Considerations

The elementary school years afford educators with some developmental advantages in addressing the needs students have for learning to be more responsible. Younger children have not engaged in unproductive thinking, feeling, and behaving for as many years as youth in secondary classes for students with EBD. Their cognitive and behavioral repertoires are still emerging. The overt behaviors exhibited result from an interaction of biological functions, developmentally determined patterns of growth, the child's learned responses, and the environment. As noted in the introduction, environment plays an important role in the facilitation of children's beliefs about themselves and their expectations of future events (Wood, 1996). Unavoidably challenging behaviors make it easy to focus on the problems students with EBD present. It is important, however, to be aware of behaviors that are age appropriate. Everything students with EBD do is not representative of their exceptionality. Being aware of the behaviors of more typically developing youth can provide insight and a measure of reassurance when examining the children you work with. Ellsworth (1996) and Wyckoff and Unell (1993) provide lists of age-normed behaviors. The lists provided in Table 1 are adapted from their work.

Having a clearer understanding of how responsible behavior develops in the general elementary-age child provides a framework for distinguishing "normal" behaviors from those that are truly deviant. In addition, the developmental stages children follow provide a direction for selecting from an array of educationally relevant strategies in supporting students' present levels of functioning and facilitating further growth. The key to modifying thoughts, emotions, and behavior lies in the daily interactions students have with each other and with significant adults.

Suggested Interventions

1. Address physiological needs through adequate food, rest, activity, lighting, temperature control, and referrals to other service providers. Students who are undernourished, in physical pain, sleepy, or ill will not be sufficiently motivated to learn (Maslow, 1962).

2. Distinguish between biologically determined traits of temperament (e.g., intensity; general mood; activity level; sensory sensitivity; regularity in sleeping, eating, and other biological functions; approach to new people and situations; adaptability) and learned behaviors when selecting target behaviors to modify. Make environmental changes and use coping strategies to address issues of temperament (Turecki, 1989). For example, a child who is biologically "wired" to be

     Developing Personal and Interpersonal Responsibility

more active than his peers cannot control the need to move. He does not have to use that energy to knock other students' blocks to the floor, run around the room during story time, or talk incessantly in class. He can be expected to refrain from destructive and disruptive behaviors. Simply telling him to sit down, reinforcing sitting, and punishing noncompliance, however, will not work. He still needs to move. Permission to stand at his desk during independent work periods, friendly challenges to jump as many times as he can in one place during play periods, and requests for his help in distributing books in preparation for story time are ways to meet his needs for movement.

The benefit of distinguishing between issues of temperament and learned behavior lies in the development of the child's sense of self as a capable learner and his or her belief that adults are understanding, caring people (Turecki, 1989). As educators shape behaviors, it is essential to remember that the way students think about themselves and the world is also being shaped. Other suggestions for addressing temperament include (a) providing less sensory stimulation for sensitive children, (b) giving students time to "warm up" to new people or experiences, and (c) providing choices of materials and activities when possible. Develop an effective behavior-modification program to stop undesirable behaviors and reinforce functional behaviors. Clearly and positively stated rules, consistently and predictably enforced, with logical, instructional, developmentally appropriate consequences are essential components of any behavior-management system (Alberto & Troutman, 1982; Turecki, 1989).

Children cannot hope to learn to exhibit responsible behavior in the absence of a safe environment. Failing to establish adequate external control prior to students' acquisition of self-control inhibits growth, encourages unproductive thinking, and teaches students to act irresponsibly. The type of self-esteem that leads to responsible behavior is not enhanced by unconditional positive regard for destructive behavior. That type of self-esteem is a byproduct of the mastery of socially sanctioned skills. Students who become successful manipulators of adults and peers in overly permissive environments may express positive feelings about their abilities to intimi-

Table 1
Age-Normed Behavior

5-Year-Old
Cooperative
May lie or steal
May boss others
Enjoys helping
Models adults
Exaggerates
Enjoys rote learning
Hypersensitive to
  little hurts
Recognizes joy
 in others

6-Year-Old
Oppositional
Brash
Tantrums easily
Extreme mood swings
Tattles
Instigates and teases
Cheats
Has to win
Thinking susceptible to
  shutting down when stressed
Recognizes pain and anger
  in others

7-Year-Old
Small setbacks cause
  work paralysis
Sad
Egocentric sense of fairness
Teases
Jealous of siblings
Confrontive, aggressive
May truly work out
  of responsibility

8-Year-Old
Shows off
Opinionated
Acts confidently, but easily hurt
Interested in money
Self-disciplined
"Black and white" sense of
  morality
More logical
Less egocentric
Wants a best friend
Fascinated with the real world

9-Year-Old
Sexual awareness
Personal dignity and
  responsibility
Recognizes fear and
  surprise in others
Procrastinates
Is forgetful
Bossiness is resented
Able to give a fair hearing
to other's opinions
Rudimentary understanding
  of cause and effect

10-Year-Old
Likes to make deals
Hot-tempered
Interested in sex
Likes clubs and group
  involvement
Learning styles emerge
Talkative
Likes democratic class meetings
Fairness evaluated in terms of
  self gain
Payback is highly valued
Competitive

Developing Personal and Interpersonal Responsibility

11-Year-Old	12-Year-Old
Ambivalent	Struggles over independence
Self-centered	and dependence
Prone to hero-worship	Bossy
Toward adults:	Preoccupied with appearance
rude	Boys resist baths
tests limits	Girls consumed with hair and
manipulative	make-up
Toward peers:	Feelings of power and
needs approval	insightfulness
susceptible to peer pressure	See themselves as authorities
Either/Or thinker	Sudden bursts of "goodness"
Obsessive-compulsive	Sense of humor emerges
	Able to take some teasing
	Mood swings are rare
	Video games and TV are passions
	Sense of humor emerges

date others. This is not, however, the desired outcome. Modifying the environment to increase students' opportunities for success is not to be confused with allowing inappropriate behavior to continue. A balance must be maintained, however, between the demands of the setting and the students' ability to comply.

3. When students are acting in responsible ways, look and sound alive. Younger children particularly enjoy dramatic and vivid language. Use impressive vocabulary, varied voice tones, and pronounced body language. When students are acting inappropriately, show as little emotion as possible. Be boring!

4. Establish routines in the classroom that facilitate a sense of purpose, balance students' needs for interactive and independent work periods, and increase students' feelings of security and control through predictable sequences of events. Students can take more responsibility for themselves when they know what to expect from others (Hewett & Taylor, 1980).

5. Avoid discussing inappropriate behavior when possible. Distracting students with a joke, story, or item of interest is often more effective than a reprimand. Changing the pace of a lesson, increasing the use of reinforcers, offering alternatives for instruction, and increasing task-focused assistance are ways to keep a positive focus and encourage more appropriate behaviors. Use Redl's (1966) techniques for managing surface behaviors. These techniques include

- Antiseptic bouncing (removal of a student from a potentially overstimulating event prior to the display of a problem).

- Proximity control (moving closer to a student without commenting on the behavior).

- Hurdle-help (offering assistance).

- Tension decontamination (humor).

- Removal of seductive objects.

- Restructuring (schedule or room arrangement changes).

- Introduction of highly engaging activities.

6. Model optimistic thinking (Seligman, 1995).

7. Use stories (Cecil & Roberts, 1992; Feder-Feitel, 1993), *curriculum* (Caputo, 1995; Moe & Pohlman, 1989; Seligman, 1995; Vernon, 1989), *and class discussions to directly teach students the vocabulary and skills necessary for more productive thinking, feeling, and behaving.* Seligman (1995) has studied extensively the mechanisms people use to develop basic orientations of optimism and pessimism. His work suggests that adults who are optimistic have better health, achieve more over the course of their lives, and persist longer when faced with obstacles. Responsible self-management is enhanced through thinking styles that (a) attribute personal control to the maintenance of positive events, (b) limit problems to specific settings, and (c) express an expectation of hope for future outcomes. While children exhibit a well-defined preference for optimistic or pessimistic thinking as early as age 7, adults can help them learn more productive ways of thinking before these patterns are well ingrained. With children younger than 10 years of age, it is important to model optimistic thinking styles when explaining a crisis or trauma to them and when providing corrective feedback.

Developing Personal and Interpersonal Responsibility

Adults should carefully explain that an event or situation such as the death of a loved one, divorce, or drug abuse is not something they caused, could have controlled, or have the power to change. Children do not have enough experience to distinguish events that are under their control from ones they have no power to control. For this reason, it is not unusual for them to blame themselves when tragedy occurs. This misunderstanding on their part can lead them to believe that they are bad. Adults need to help them make that distinction and be sensitive to any expression of guilt that is not warranted. In addition, they need to be reassured that support systems are still in place and that the future can and will be better. When children make mistakes, they need

- A clear explanation of what is expected in such situations.

- An acknowledgment of the appropriate behaviors exhibited even in the midst of the incident under discussion.

- A statement of belief in their ability to perform successfully in the future.

If students are over the age of 10, Seligman (1995) advocates directly teaching the skills necessary to (a) recognize unproductive thinking, (b) dispute and modify the self-talk, and (c) act on the new belief. Using EIlis's work on Rational-Emotive Therapy, Bernard (1990), DiGuiseppe and Bernard (1990), and Vernon (1989) provide further information on helping students to modify the thoughts that drive emotions and behavior. A variety of affective curriculum materials are currently available to help students learn more productive ways of thinking about themselves and others.

8. *Teach social skills that are attainable given students' developmental level and biological attributes.* Braaten (1995) has developed the *Behavioral Objective Sequence* that provides a scope and sequence of developmentally aligned behaviors across six subscales. The subscales include adaptive functioning, task behaviors, self-management, personal skills, interpersonal skills, and communication. Success is the most powerful motivator available. Selecting behaviors in a developmentally sensitive sequence allows students to experience more immediate success and build upon newly acquired skills as they mature. Curriculum materials can then be used during social

skills instruction to greater benefit. Mannix (1989), McGinnis & Goldstein (1984), and Schmidt and Friedman (1991) are representative of many authors of social skill curricula for use with students in the elementary grades.

9. Use instructional strategies that are success oriented and aligned with the children's cognitive developmental level. Precision Teaching (Lindsley, 1990) and direct instruction (Rosenshine, 1989) facilitate mastery of knowledge level skills. Attention to students' modality preferences can also increase motivation, time on task, and learning (Carbo, 1997). Elementary students develop a sense of industry (Erikson, 1963) through academic achievement. Patterns of frustration and failure established in the first years of schooling are difficult to change later. Personal and interpersonal responsibility requires a belief in the efficacy of one's efforts. For this reason, care should be taken to avoid curriculum materials and instructional strategies that are not well suited to the functioning level of the student. Even well-documented methods such as cooperative learning (Slavin, 1990) must be evaluated with particular students' needs in mind. If prerequisite social skills and self-control have not been established, give the student or group alternative assignments (Rockwell, 1996; Rockwell & Guetzloe, 1996).

10. Look for ways to engage each student with materials that he or she prefers and provide choices daily. If the objective is to learn spelling words, for example, offer a variety of methods for practicing them. Stencils, typing, cut-and-paste activities, writing them with markers, forming the words with clay, using cookie-cutter letters in dough, drawing letters in shaving cream or pudding, and gluing alphabet macaroni to cardboard represent several alternatives to writing the words on notebook paper. Establishing a habit of participation and responsible task completion is easier to accomplish when tasks are engaging.

11. Find ways to showcase students' work. Students need to get as much recognition out of work done well as possible. Put their work on display in the hall, office, media center, or cafeteria. Leave post-it notes for staff to use in writing comments about the work.

 Developing Personal and Interpersonal Responsibility

12. *Encourage students to move from a more egocentric orientation to identification with the group by providing academic and recreational opportunities for making personal contributions to class projects* (Rockwell, 1996; Rockwell & Guetzloe, 1996). Anthologies of students' writings, a class photograph album, and a bulletin board display that each student helped to create are a few examples.

13. *Make use of affective bulletin boards.* Seasonal or academic themes can be used to showcase responsible choices made throughout the day. During the fall, for example, a large tree can be posted on a wall in the classroom. A banner titled "The Apples of My Eye" can be printed above the tree. The teacher can place a construction paper apple on the desk of students whenever they exhibit responsible behavior. The student can write his or her name on the apple and write a word or phrase to document the positive behavior. Apples can be added to the tree at the end of each day. At the end of the month or instructional unit, students can be given construction paper to make a tree of their own. All the apples that belong to them can be pasted to their tree and taken home to share with their families.

14. *When the group is ready, make use of group contingencies.* Use charts, paper chains, or some other method for recording individual's contributions to the group goal. Recently, a teacher (Chris Sandel of the Calvin A. Hunsinger School described in the introduction) agreed to let the second graders "fix" her hair if everyone earned a targeted number of points on his or her point cards for two consecutive days. Once the class met their goal, the teacher was treated to a gel and toothpaste plaster. She spent the day with her short hair twisted into several irregular spikes. Everyone in the school enjoyed the event. The students received extra benefits from the reactions of others in the hall and cafeteria. Humor proved to be a powerful motivator!

15. *Provide students with developmentally appropriate job assignments in the classroom.* Frieberg (1996) describes a program that engages the students in generating lists of jobs for problems that occur throughout the day. In one elementary class, for example, constant interruptions in line walking due to untied shoe laces created

frequent delays. The class decided to appoint a person responsible for tying shoe laces. Even very young students can be given jobs such as turning off the lights when the class leaves the room; watering plants; carrying the teacher's clipboard; or stacking books in the reading corner. Assign jobs on a rotating basis, or allow students to purchase jobs with points if the class uses a point system.

16. Increase ownership and responsibility through student input into behavioral and academic evaluation processes (Glasser, 1985; Schneider, 1996). Students can be taught to assist in establishing criteria, generating suggestions for improvement, and assessing progress through group and individual monitoring procedures. Students who may not be able to assume full responsibility for some behaviors and levels of achievement do benefit from the shared experience of being part of a successful group. The teacher should structure these experiences carefully in the beginning to ensure mastery.

One third-grade teacher at the Calvin A. Hunsinger School, Barbara Hartley, decided to let the class help set criteria for poor, good, and excellent writing assignments. Together, students and teacher defined an excellent paper as one that followed all the rules of writing conventions that they had been taught; made sense; covered the topic; and included a decorative, hand-colored border. Good papers had only a few errors and no border. Poor papers had several errors, were messy, and did not make sense. As they continued to use their system of evaluation throughout the year, the teacher reported increased academic skills in writing as well as a greater willingness on the part of students to go for quality status in their work. Behavioral applications of this process might include group-established norms for keeping the classroom materials in order or time limits on the use of certain favored materials.

17. Begin to engage in service-learning projects with students as soon as their behaviors are sufficiently under control. They need the sense of power, achievement, and productivity that giving to others provides. Emery and Turpin (1996) describe a service project that engaged elementary school students in writing and decorating cards for elderly clients in a nursing home. Their model for developing service-learning projects stresses the importance of integrating service learning with academic themes, student-relevant goals and objectives, and community needs. When projects are planned with the strengths of the students in mind, methods for involving everyone regardless of their functioning level can be found. Service-learning projects have the advantage of providing students with authentic, community-based reasons for acquiring academic and behavioral skills.

18. Invite clubs from the community into the classroom and school. Boy Scouts of America has an affective curriculum that can be used with boys and girls. Instead of badges, students earn stickers as they work through the various lessons. 4-H offers an academic curriculum as well. Students in classes for EBD often lack experience with community-based peer groups. Holding club meetings in the school during school hours allows club sponsors the benefit of having trained assistance with potential behavioral problems and gives students an opportunity to participate in an age-appropriate activity. At the Calvin A. Hunsinger School, the elementary scout troop is responsible for conducting the honor guard for the American flag at all formal assemblies. The students who are involved take great pride in their status as Boy Scouts.

19. Engage students in a mini-business. As early as the second or third grade, students begin to have an interest in earning money. Projects can include services such as collating and stapling papers or products such as computer-generated cards and banners. One group in a third-grade class for students with EBD made and sold small paper cups of frozen fruit flavored drinks. Prior to beginning the business, the teacher discussed possible projects with them. The project selected had to be easy enough for children of that age to complete, stay within the budget allowed, require only equipment available in the school, and provide a desired product or service. The students conducted a market survey during lunch periods, charted the results, and got to work. To limit the amount of time and work required, the frozen treats were only available on Fridays. Students helped keep bank registers, ordered supplies, produced the frozen treats, conducted the sales, and made a group decision about what to do with the profits.

20. Collaborate with more than one class to practice and reinforce targeted social skills. Hold regular reinforcing events that reward students for cooperation rather than competition. The Calvin A. Hunsinger staff conducted a field-day event titled "Go for the Gold." Each student was given a laminated Olympic medal on a ribbon to wear to the event. As students worked together and used the social skills being taught in the classrooms each day, they received stars to put on their medals. Stars represented successful participation as evidenced by the use of responsible behavior. Some of the activities included playing with a parachute and working together to solve written clues that led to an ice chest with popsicles in it. Students and teachers had the added benefit of enjoying each other's company in a nonacademic setting.

Opportunities to play are an important part of the process of mastering appropriate behaviors and learning to expect positive outcomes. Teaching children with EBD to have fun in group settings is an important but often overlooked process. Peer group involvement becomes increasingly more important as children mature. The ability to form and maintain productive relationships with adults and peers is crucial in the eventual maintenance of a responsible lifestyle.

Conclusion

A brief description of a former student is offered as a final illustration of the complex issues involved in the teaching of personal and interpersonal responsibility. One Tuesday morning several years ago, I received a new student into my primary-level, self-contained class for students with EBD.

Joe (a fictitious name) was 7 years old and had just been released from a university-based psychiatric facility in another county. No one from that facility or from his home had contacted me. A social worker simply dropped by the classroom the day before his arrival to give a brief description of his case. He was placed in the custody of his grandparents at the age of 6 months because his mother was addicted to drugs and had severely neglected him. He did not smile for several months and had frequent, violent, and unprovoked tantrums. The grandparents sought professional help when he began to verbalize his intent to kill animals and people. The incident that prompted referral to the hospital was Joe's attempt to kill his grandparents while they slept by setting fire to the house. He scored in the gifted range on individually administered intelligence tests so his inability to act responsibly was not a function of poor cognitive skills.

On that first Tuesday morning, he greeted me politely and participated calmly and appropriately in class activities for the first 2 hours. Then without warning or noticeable provocation, he began violently banging his head on a brick wall, scraping his face with his fingernails, and smashing any materials within his reach. His screams were ear-splitting and relentless. I sent my associate to another room with the other students and attempted to calm him. While on the floor cradling his head to prevent further damage from self-imposed blows and restraining his attempts to scratch himself and me, the principal entered the room. He towered over the two of us and demanded that I make Joe stop screaming. I explained over the howling that I could not do that. The principal became irate. The general-education class of second-grade students next door were terribly frightened, and their teacher had asked the principal to intervene. I was told that I needed to instruct my students in responsible, school-appropriate behavior. I promised that I would do that as soon as Joe stopped yelling and trying to destroy himself. Over the course of the next 18 months, Joe did indeed become a responsible member of the school and eventually was transferred to a school for students with superior gifts and talents.

Joe's story illustrates the multiple, interacting variables that teachers with students who have EBD must understand. Some of Joe's behavior was related to temperament. Other behaviors were learned. He had frightened people often enough in the past to know that it sometimes achieved a useful purpose — people would demand less and give more. In addition to learned and biologically controlled responses, Joe exhibited advanced cognitive abilities. While this was helpful in redirecting Joe's energy to more productive, achievement-oriented academic and behavioral goals, it also worked against him in establishing peer relationships in certain situations. The environment of the self-contained classroom provided him with the structure and safety he needed through clearly defined limits, immediate consequences, predictable and balanced scheduling of activities, social skills instruction, and academic tasks modified for his level of cognitive functioning.

As he required less external support, expectations for his participation in problem-solving sessions and cooperative-learning activities increased. Joe began to ask permission to visit the media center and general education classrooms unattended. He made friends with peers in other classrooms and was a welcome member of the school community. His grandparents reported that he was also making excellent progress at home, in counseling, and in community-based youth programs. Collaborative, developmentally sensitive, and individually modified interventions helped Joe gain new skills and reframe his beliefs about himself and those around him. School, friends, family, and neighborhood experiences became increasingly reinforcing. Joe was well on his way to developing the personal and interpersonal responsibility he needed for a healthy, productive life.

The Secondary School Years 3

Adolescence presents its own constellation of challenges for youth. Havighurst (1952) outlined the developmental tasks adolescents face in terms of the skills and knowledge required for a successful transition from childhood to full adult status in the larger community. Functional adults are expected to exhibit several competencies:

- The ability to form mature relationships.

- An acceptance of their physiques.

- An acceptance of their sex role.

- Emotional independence.

- Economic independence.

- Preparation for a vocation.

- Preparation for family life.

- Civic competence.

- Socially acceptable and responsible behavior.

- Maintenance of a socially acceptable system of values and ethics.

Educational programs must address the dynamic and increasingly urgent needs of youth with EBD. Adolescents with EBD often age-out or drop out of the protective systems of care available to them long before they have demonstrated mastery of the competencies just listed. Time will not permit unidimensional approaches for teaching the essential components of personal and interpersonal responsibility. The school's responsibility includes developing a positive school climate and establishing links among the various resources present in the school, home, and community. Effectively responding to the specific needs of secondary-level students with EBD requires addressing various key factors (Guetzloe, 1996):

- Positive adult models who are knowledgeable, respectful, prepared, confident, firm, fair, patient, truthful, and committed to society.

- A physically and psychologically safe environment.

- Reasonable rules, expectations, routines, and schedules.

- A positive behavior-management system that is rich in reinforcement and is consistent and success oriented.

- Individualized, attainable, and measurable goals and objectives.

- Relevant curriculum and age-appropriate instructional materials given the individual needs of students and the tasks of adolescence.

- Effective, humane, and positive instructional techniques.

- Opportunities for socialization in the total school environment as well as in the community.

- Parental involvement.

- Community-based instruction.

A variety of programs have been developed to address the needs of youth. Hetfield (1994) reports on the benefits of group ownership for students with EBD in the production of a school newspaper. Ward and Conderman (1995) and Rockwell (1996) describe economics activities that prepare students for decisions about budgeting and purchasing items on credit. McWhirter and Bloom (1994) and Patton, de la Garza, and Harmon (1997) extend the secondary curriculum to include employability skills that aid students in the transition from school to work. Watkins and Wilkes (1993) and Sodac (1997) document the power of belonging to clubs and organizations devoted to service learning in the community as a means for assisting students in building responsible attitudes and enriching relationships beyond the school campus. The Foxfire approach (Ensminger & Dangel, 1992) serves as an additional model of excellence in the search for ways to engage youth with EBD in the complex tasks of developing mature, responsible life styles.

The staff at the Calvin A. Hunsinger School are working to extend the options available to students at the secondary level. Over the years, various programs have come and gone in response to the particular needs of the students served within the system. Slowly the realization is dawning that there is no one answer — no silver bullets exist. The ideas and solutions offered here are representative of an ever evolving pattern of growth. The individual talents and needs of students and staff, the resources as well as the limitations of the larger systems that surround the school, the input of parents and other professionals, theory, and research are reflected in the daily applications described in this chapter. Brendtro, Brokenleg, and Bockern (1990) stress the importance of structuring programs for youth with regular opportunities to form attachments, demonstrate mastery, exercise autonomy, and provide a service to others. Embedded in these programs are the essential elements that Havighurst (1952), Guetzloe (1996), Brendtro et al. (1990), and others have identified.

A Center Approach: Responsive Programming

At the Calvin A. Hunsinger School, the staff strives to create a cooperative and compassionate environment where students can learn and, among other things, solve problems. Program goals reflect the staff's desire to instill in the students a yearning to celebrate life, embrace diversity, and develop a strong work ethic. The following middle-school and high-school-level components represent opportunities students have to learn self-reliance, responsibility, and a general preparedness for life.

The Programs

Each program in the following section illustrates successful ways to encourage students to (a) establish positive relationships with peers and adults; (b) demonstrate mastery in social, emotional, and cognitive domains; (c) develop productive outlets for meeting their needs for power, control, fun, and independence; and (d) explore a range of academic and vocational domains within protective boundaries. The factors that characterize effective programs for adolescents with EBD are embedded in the guiding principles as well as the daily practice of these initiatives.

Therapeutic Recreation

The recreation program was developed by a behavior specialist and was designed to improve student skills in the areas of cooperation, listening, following directions, respecting rules, leadership, acceptance of others' differences, compassion, encouragement of others, and self-reliance. Through games, activities, sports, and team-building events, this program has proven to be very successful. All students are welcomed to recreation regardless of their athletic abilities or skill levels. Students are required to complete their class assignments and homework and maintain acceptable behavior in order to attend recreation on any given day.

Students have taken responsibility for developing the outcomes and qualities needed for a successful recreation program. Giving students ownership in the program is utilized as a method to improve behavior. Changes become intrinsic when rules and consequences are managed by peers rather than staff. Choice has become a word that students use in communicating with one another. When a student fails to follow the correct path toward a desired outcome, peers say, "We don't need that here. If you choose to continue, you are choosing to go inside." The program belongs to the students. This instills a stronger sense of pride in what they are able to accomplish.

If a member of the group is not participating properly, the other students feel comfortable letting that student know that the behavior is unacceptable. Peer pressure is generally more effective than adult control, as evidenced by the decreased number of students sent into the building during this activity. In addition to the benefits of positive peer pressure, some students have emerged as leaders. Students who often have a difficult time in class with issues of adult authority find more productive ways to channel their anger and energy. Another program called Wolf Pack was developed to address the needs of these students.

The Wolf Pack

The Wolf Pack was designed to teach and enhance the leadership skills of students with EBD. The name of the group was chosen because humans like wolves need to be taught skills that will help them survive and function in society. Wolves are very social animals; they are extremely loyal, choose to mate for life, and are strongly committed to the survival of the pack. These animals demonstrate the utmost trust and caring for one another. They depend on each other for food, protection, nurturing, and the raising of the pups. These qualities are absolutely essential for the entire community to survive. As the pups grow into adolescence, they are taught the necessary survival and cooperation skills (Savage, 1988).

In contrast, the faces of our students tell the stories of children who have not had the opportunity to experience the happiness, fun, love, and security that directs one along the path which encourages growth. The violence that these children have experienced has forced them to become seasoned soldiers in the war against poverty, drugs, hate, and fear. Physical aggression is often the only form of communication they know. They literally fight to stay alive in a community that holds no love for them (Schmidt & Friedman, 1991).

The curriculum for the Wolf Pack was created to integrate the affective skills, trust building, conflict resolution, and Native American culture. It is modeled after the kinship the wolves experience in their packs.

To ensure the pack's survival and to create an atmosphere that will motivate students to improve in all aspects of their lives, the Wolf Pack members must adhere to particular expectations and guidelines. To be eligible for the group, all Wolf Pack members must

- Maintain mastery-level performance of specifically targeted behaviors.

- Maintain a minimum of a "B" average.

- Attend Friday Wolf Pack meetings during the school day.

- Remain eligible to participate in recreation 4 out of 5 days.

- Select a new job every 6 weeks.

- Assist the Alpha wolves during recreation, field days, field trips, camping trips, and other special activities planned by the pack.

When a student becomes a member of the Wolf Pack, he is given the status of "pup." The pup is then guided and trained within the group to be dependable and to earn the trust of the other Wolf Pack members. As the pup learns and grows, she is invited to serve as a cocaptain during recreation periods. The training and guidance allows the students to master the skills required to successfully complete their duties, which positively influences students' self-esteem and self-respect. In time, they begin to work together for the good of the pack. It is our experience that students who have participated in the Wolf Pack program are more likely to transition to general education schools and with a higher rate of success.

Camping

The sense of belonging fostered through the recreation and Wolf Pack programs have led to the development of a camping program. Camping experiences allow staff and students for a few days to work, play, and learn together as a family. In a tranquil and beautiful atmosphere, the rough exterior of the students begins to fade. Social skills, responsibility, and trust are enhanced as the group works together to prepare meals and other activities. Being dependable as an individual has a direct effect on the functioning of the family group. Being interdependent requires a balance between meeting personal needs and responding cooperatively to others' needs. Eating, sleeping, playing, exploring, and sharing as a family brings the lessons of interdependence into clear focus for students.

   Developing Personal and Interpersonal Responsibility

Every evening after a walk through the woods, the group sits around the campfire to talk about the day and to share feelings. Students and staff laugh, cry, act silly, and openly share dreams, hopes, and thoughts in an atmosphere that protects against feeling fearful, guilty, or inferior. The students are comfortable enough to act like children. Sadly, this is often the first time in their young lives that they have experienced the strength and encouragement to do so. For those few days, the group of staff and students functions as a family. More is accomplished during one trip to the wilderness than staff had ever thought possible. A desire to bring some of the lessons learned in the woods back to the school has led to the creation of a conflict-resolution and peer-mediation program.

Conflict Resolution

Students are introduced to the idea of conflict resolution through the use of peace tables. These tables are established as safe zones for discussion of clashes between students. Identifying feelings, taking responsibility for choices, and learning to value the feelings of others can be fostered in a safe, nonthreatening environment (Abrams, 1993). The middle school staff has found conflict resolution to be a viable option in teaching students to accept individual differences and to solve problems through communication rather than through violence. In addition to including conflict resolution in the middle-school curriculum, an affective program has been developed because students at this level need information as well as skills. The following description of the staff's response to these needs highlights areas of concern and activities designed to address students' needs.

Affective Instruction

Finding a method for sharing information with middle school students with EBD was the staff's first challenge. Initially, anger-management groups were attempted within each classroom setting. However, many students were not comfortable disclosing personal thoughts and feelings in front of their peers. They feared that their peers would use the information against them at a later date. Despite efforts to develop the appropriate group dynamics in the classrooms, the setting continued to be too threatening for some students.

The staff began to shift the format for affective lessons to less personally threatening activities. Facts, statistics, true life stories, various speakers, and discussions driven by students' questions proved to be more successful. The first year, assemblies were planned around relevant topics such as drugs, alcohol, AIDS, and sexually transmitted diseases. Rules for behavior during assemblies were reviewed each day. Students who were not able to behave appropriately were asked to recognize that they were not ready and request permission to leave. Those students who did not leave on their own were escorted from the assembly by staff. The majority of students enjoyed this format for learning and participated willingly by asking questions, giving their opinions, and sharing information of their own. Assemblies, guest speakers, and videos proved to be less threatening than more intense and personal classroom discussions.

Much has happened during the development of the program. Students have accepted responsibility for preparing the assembly room by setting up chairs and arriving on time. Students have also been asked to provide feedback to staff about their likes and dislikes. As a result, more guest speakers were added to the program during the second year of development. Students were also encouraged to become involved through prizes for attendance and participation. The best overall performer was awarded a ticket to Disney World or Busch Gardens. The runner-up was awarded a T-shirt with a Disney character of his or her choice.

In addition to assemblies, essays and poster contests related to particular topics each grading period were added. This encouraged students to get involved with the available literature on a more personal level. Videos and other resources could be accessed through the school media center and other sources provided by the social worker assigned to the middle school team.

During the third year of operation, students were encouraged to retain information by incorporating an Affective Jeopardy game into the annual activity package. Students worked together as classroom teams to answer questions presented to them on the various topics covered each grading period. Teachers had a notebook that served as a resource manual throughout the year. Pretests and posttests were given as a method to assess growth. The test questions along with vocabulary lists and discussion topics were also representative of the information classroom teams should have during the "Super Bowl playoffs." The success of this portion of the program has prompted students and staff to continue and to expand the competition.

Topics for the affective program are covered and presented in different formats. Speakers will often ask for class participation, share life stories, do demonstrations, ask for role plays, vote, share opinions, or debate a topic. Variety makes a difference because each speaker offers something unique. For example, one guest who talked with the students about AIDS was the same age as the students. Of all the speakers the students have heard, this person evoked the most response. The students made him a giant card to demonstrate their support for his fight against the disease.

The affective program begins the second 6 weeks of school and runs through the fifth 6-week grading period. Classes need the first and last grading periods for goal setting and goal evaluation. During the first 6 weeks, students complete the Piers-Harris Children's Self-Concept Scale (Piers & Harris, 1969), participate in a bridge building competition, and set personal goals for the year. After the winter break, students use the 3 weeks left in the first semester to evaluate progress they have made and complete posters, essays, or bumper stickers. The affective program ends in the spring with a Multicultural Fair. Each class selects a country and prepares a presentation to share with the other classes. Students might do a food demonstration, a play, a dance, or just share facts. During the last 6 weeks, students complete another Piers-Harris Self-Concept Scale (Piers & Harris, 1969) and reevaluate their goals.

Topics covered during a recent school year include

- Orientation: Understanding Adolescence.
- Nutrition.
- Smoking.
- Drugs.
- Alcohol.
- Human Sexuality.
- Sexually Transmitted Diseases/AIDS.
- Stress Management for the Holidays (or Anytime).
- Citizenship/Patriotism/Rights.
- Ethics/Values.
- Decision Making.
- Self-Esteem.
- Dealing with Emotions.
- Friendship and Dating
- Peer Pressure.
- Resolving Conflicts/Domestic Violence.
- Peer Mediation.
- Preventing Violence/Gangs.
- Multiculturalism.

The use of community speakers and resources in conjunction with assemblies, classroom-level discussions, and school-wide events has allowed students and staff to tackle difficult topics in a more open and comfortable format. These efforts have demanded a tremendous investment of time and energy from the social worker, the middle school teachers, and other staff members. As the number of students in the center increases, the needs presented to the staff increase as well. However, the positive responses from the majority of the students involved encourage the staff to persevere in these areas. Because of the program's popularity and success, the high school staff has developed a parallel program around the same topics.

   Developing Personal and Interpersonal Responsibility

Work and Responsible Self-Management

The secondary-level teachers at Calvin A. Hunsinger School continue to look for ways to involve students in meaningful work and vocation-related experiences. Some students attend school part of the day and work in community-based programs for course credit for the remainder of each school day. Assistance is provided to groups of high school students in finding various entry level jobs in area businesses. Students complete academic work at school and receive course credit for vocational training through participation in a paid community-based job.

Another group of students need a sheltered workshop experience as a prerequisite to a job in an area business setting. These students complete academic training at school and ride a bus with the teacher and classroom associate to the Abilities Program. Staff at Abilities work collaboratively with Hunsinger staff to teach students to follow typical procedures such as the use of a time clock, keeping paperwork related to work assignments, following the directions of a boss, and remaining on task with the piecework items required each day. Students complete a variety of jobs such as assembling pens, collating and stapling, or stuffing envelopes for mailing. Paychecks are earned according to the number of tasks completed each day.

Another teacher has combined her love of horses with her talent for teaching secondary level students with EBD in an equine-oriented program she calls Project R.I.D.E. Equine activities develop self-awareness, build self-confidence, improve concentration, and increase self-discipline. The vocational component of the program introduces students to careers in the horse industry. *The Dictionary of Occupational Titles* (U.S. Department of Labor, 1991) lists 26 vocations from stable manager to Equine Veterinarian Technician related to the care and management of horses. In order for students to earn course credit through these activities, a classroom instruction component is required. Classroom course work includes

- Equine anatomy and conformation.
- Breeding and bloodlines.

- Equine parasites and disease.

- Lameness.

- General care and maintenance.

- Bookkeeping and budgeting.

- Riding tack and its use.

- Buying and selling horses.

As with the affective program, guest speakers are brought to the classroom or stable to discuss the details of managing various jobs such as equine veterinarian, equine dentist, blacksmith (farrier), stable/racetrack groom, professional horse transporter, and member of the sheriff's mounted posse. The curriculum is designed to allow students to earn credit in vocational or exceptional education courses under state guidelines.

The stable-management component of the program includes hands-on work with the horses. Students are responsible for the general care of the horses. They gain knowledge in the feeding, watering, and daily maintenance of the horses. They must be ready at all times to answer questions about the confirmation, temperature, respiration, soundness, and water intake of the horses assigned to their care. Students are also observed in the general grooming of their horses.

Another goal of this program is to assist students in the transition from school to work. Preparing students for eventual participation in employment, family, and community life requires staff to focus on activities and objectives that support students' growth in those directions. A variety of instructional strategies, methods, and materials are used to enhance the transition process. Examples of the techniques and assignments used in this program include

- Employability-focused textbooks.

- Business-oriented projects that integrate academics with life skills.

- Student portfolio development.

     Developing Personal and Interpersonal Responsibility

- Instructional units that include local community resource information.

- Participation in equine-oriented organizations such as the American Horse Show Association or 4-H Clubs.

- Practicum experiences with prospective employers.

The combination of classroom instruction, relevant curriculum, hands-on experiences, community-based opportunities, and collaboration among agencies improves the variety of options available to students, the quality of programming, and the successful outcomes for those involved. While the Abilities Program, Project R.I.D.E., and the work-study program meet the needs of many students, others are better served in different ways.

Other programs available to students include a student-operated lunch service, which is provided two or three times a week for staff. The food service class learns to cook, budget, and serve through this in-house mini-business. Another group of students is taken to the local Pinellas Technical Education Center for vocational training for part of the school day. Students spend the remainder of each day completing academic course requirements at Hunsinger.

In addition to these secondary options, two other teachers assist a group of middle-school students in a mini-business conducted during sixth period. Students must complete all academic assignments and exhibit responsible behavior in order to be eligible to participate each day. Academic course work is developed around 13 career strand options over the school year. The class spends approximately 3 weeks studying each career strand through literature, research projects, math assignments, science, social studies, field trips, and guest speakers. Students have stopped asking why they must learn certain types of information. The relevance of the academic curriculum as well as the social skills required for successful group participation are clearly linked to the world of work for these students. They are welcomed at a neighboring school when they visit to share and sell their products. Guest speakers and business partners in the community find this group to be well prepared with reasonable and insightful questions.

Conclusion 4

The programs described in this monograph illustrate some of the many worthy attempts the Hunsinger staff and others like them are making to increase achievement and encourage responsible behavior of students with EBD. The key to success with any of the programs lies, however, in the ability of staff and students to build relationships through the productive attainment of mutually agreeable goals. The programs for students at Calvin A. Hunsinger School emerge from the needs of the students. When a program has met a need and is no longer necessary, teachers, administrators, and support staff work with students to develop new options.

Being responsible requires a sensitivity to the issues present in a situation along with a willingness to respond in a reasonable manner. We feel strongly that the most effective way to teach responsibility to youth of any age is to model it. The programs discussed here share a commitment to and a core belief in responsible action on behalf of students with EBD, a commitment demonstrated through thoughts, words, and deeds.

References 5

Abrams, G. (1993). *The training institute: Conflict resolution, mediation, and peace.* Miami Beach, FL: The Peace Education Foundation.

Alberto, P. A., & Troutman, A. C. (1982). *Applied behavior analysis for teachers: Influencing student performance.* Columbus, OH: Charles E. Merrill.

Bernard, M. E. (1990). Rational-emotive therapy with children and adolescents: Treatment strategies. *School Psychology Review, 19*(3), 294-303.

Braaten, S. (1995). *The behavioral objective sequence.* Arden Hills, MN: Institute for Adolescents with Behavioral Disorders.

Brendtro, L., Brokenleg, M., & Bochern, S. V. (1990). *Reclaiming youth at risk: Our hope for the future.* Bloomington, IN: National Education Service.

Caputo, R. A. (1995). Puppets, problem-solving and rational emotive therapy. *Beyond Behavior, 6*(2), 6-12.

Carbo, M. (1997). Reading styles times twenty. *Educational Leadership, 54*(6), 38-42.

Cecil, N. L., & Roberts, P. L. (1992). *Developing resiliency through children's literature: A guide for teachers and librarians, K-8.* Jefferson, NC: McFarland.

DiGuiseppe, R., & Bernard, M. E. (1990). The application of rational-emotive theory and therapy to school-aged children. *School Psychology Review, 19*(3), 268-286.

Edelman, M. W. (1992). *The measure of our success: A letter to my children and yours.* Boston: Beacon.

Ellsworth, J. (1996). "PEPSI": A screening and programming tool for understanding the whole child. *Teaching Exceptional Children, 29*(2), 33-44.

Emery, M., & Turpin, S. R. (1996). Service learning: Making the community connection. *Beyond Behavior, 7*(1), 15-19.

Ensminger, E. E., & Dangel, H. L. (1992). The foxfire pedagogy: A confluence of best practices for special education. *Focus on Exceptional Children, 27*(7), 1-15.

Erikson, E. H. (1963). *Childhood and society.* New York: W. W. Norton.

Feder-Feitel, L. (1993). Tough to teach topic: Teaching values. *Creative Classroom, 8*(2), 43-52.

Frieberg, H. J. (1996). From tourists to citizens in the classroom. *Educational Leadership, 54*(1), 32-36.

Glasser, W. (1985). *Control theory in the classroom.* New York: Perennial Library.

Guetzloe, E. C. (1996). Strategies that work for adolescents with emotional/behavioral disorders: Conditions, curriculum, and consequences. In L. M. Bullock & R. A. Gable (Eds.), *Best practices for managing adolescents with emotional/behavioral disorders within the school environment* (pp. 6-13). Reston, VA: The Council for Children with Behavioral Disorders.

Havighurst, R. J. (1952). *Developmental tasks and education* (2nd ed.). New York : Longmans, Green.

Hetfield, P. (1994). Using a student newspaper to motivate students with behavior disorders. *Teaching Exceptional Children, 26*(2), 6-9.

Hewett, F. M., & Taylor, F. D. (1980). *The emotionally disturbed child in the classroom: The orchestration of success* (2nd ed.). Boston: Allyn and Bacon.

Lindsley, O. R. (1990). Precision teaching: By teachers for children. *Teaching Exceptional Children, 22*(3), 10-15.

Mannix, D. (1989). *Social skills activities for special children.* West Nyack, NY: The Center for Applied Research in Education.

Maslow, A. (1962). *Toward a psychology of being.* Princeton, NJ: D. Van Nostrand.

McGinnis, E., & Goldstein, A. P. (1984). *Skillstreaming the elementary school child.* Champaign, IL: Research Press.

McWhirter, C. C., & Bloom, L. A. (1994). The effects of a student-operated business curriculum on the on-task behavior of students with behavioral disorders. *Behavioral Disorders, 19* (2), 136-141.

Moe, J., & Pohlman, D. (1989). *Kid's power: Healing games for children of alcoholics.* Redwood City, CA: Health Communications.

Patton, P. L., de la Garza, B., & Harmon, C. (1997). Employability skills + adult agency support + family support + on-the-job support = successful employment. *Teaching Exceptional Children, 29*(3), 4-10.

Piers, E. V., & Harris, D. B. (1969). *The Piers-Harris children's self-concept scale.* Los Angeles: Western Psychological Services.

Redl, F. (1966). *When we deal with children.* New York: Free Press.

Rockwell, S. (1996). *Back off, cool down, try again: Teaching students how to control aggressive behavior.* Reston, VA: The Council for Exceptional Children.

Rockwell, S., & Guetzloe, E. (1996). Group development for students with emotional/behavioral disorders. *Teaching Exceptional Children, 29*(1), 38-43.

Rosenshine, B. (1986). Synthesis of research on explicit teaching. *Educational Leadership, 43*(7), 60-69.

Savage, C. (1988). *Wolves.* San Francisco, CA: Sierra Club Books.

Schmidt, F., & Friedman, A. (1991). *Creative conflict solving for kids.* Miami Beach, FL: The Peace Education Foundation.

Schneider, E. (1996). Giving students a voice in the classroom. *Educational Leadership, 54*(1), 22-26.

Seligman, M. (1995). *The optimistic child*. New York: Bantam Books.

Slavin, R. E. (1990). *Cooperative learning theory, research, and practice*. Englewood Cliffs, NJ: Prentice Hall.

Sodac, D. G. (1997). Join the amicus club! Increasing high schoolers' social skills in an after-school program. *Teaching Exceptional Children, 29*(3), 64-67.

Turecki, S. (1989). *The difficult child*. New York: Bantam Books.

U.S. Department of Labor. (1991). *Dictionary of occupational titles* (4th ed.). Lanham, MD: Bonan Press.

Vernon, A. (1989). *Thinking, feeling, behaving, 1-6*. Champaign, IL: Research Press.

Ward, V., & Conderman, G. (1995). Rent to own: Will it bow your budget? *Teaching Exceptional Children, 28*(1), 73-75.

Watkins, J., & Wilkes, D. (1993). *Promising service-learning programs*. Greensboro, NC: South Eastern Regional Vision for Education (SERVE).

Wood, F. (1996). Life stories and behavior change. *Beyond Behavior, 7*(1), 8-14.

Wyckoff, L., & Unell, B. (1993). *How to discipline your six to twelve year old ... without losing your mind*. New York: Main Street Books, Doubleday.